3 Look at the number words and what they mean. What do you notice about each word?

6 – six 6th – sixth

Word	Meaning
sextuple	six times as much
hexagon	a flat shape with six equal sides
sextuplets	six children born at the same time
sextet	six singers or musicians

1	2	3	4	5	6	7	8	9	10
11	12	13	14	15	16	17	18	19	20
21	22	23	24	25	26	27	28	29	30
31	32	33	34	35	36	37	38	39	40
41	42	43	44	45	46	47	48	49	50
51	52	53	54	55	56	57	58	59	60
61	62	63	64	65	66	67	68	69	70
71	72	73	74	75	76	77	78	79	80
81	82	83	84	85	86	87	88	89	90
91	92	93	94	95	96	97	98	99	100

The numbers in green show the six times table. What is the pattern of the numbers in the green squares?

4 What pattern can you see on the number grid?

A catalogue record for this book is available from the British Library

Published by Ladybird Books Ltd
80 Strand, London, WC2R 0RL
A Penguin Company

2 4 6 8 10 9 7 5 3 1
© LADYBIRD BOOKS LTD MMIV. This edition MMIX
LADYBIRD and the device of a Ladybird are trademarks of Ladybird Books Ltd

ISBN: 978-140930-222-3

Printed in China

HOMEWORK HELPERS

Times Tables for School

Illustrated by Ian Cunliffe

1 Times Table

$$0 \times 1 = 0$$
$$1 \times 1 = 1$$
$$2 \times 1 = 2$$
$$3 \times 1 = 3$$
$$4 \times 1 = 4$$
$$5 \times 1 = 5$$
$$6 \times 1 = 6$$
$$7 \times 1 = 7$$
$$8 \times 1 = 8$$
$$9 \times 1 = 9$$
$$10 \times 1 = 10$$
$$11 \times 1 = 11$$
$$12 \times 1 = 12$$

One naughty elephant!

1 – one 1st – first

Word	Meaning
single	one, on its own
unicycle	one-wheeled cycle
solo	for one person
once	one time

1	2	3	4	5	6	7	8	9	10
11	12	13	14	15	16	17	18	19	20
21	22	23	24	25	26	27	28	29	30
31	32	33	34	35	36	37	38	39	40
41	42	43	44	45	46	47	48	49	50
51	52	53	54	55	56	57	58	59	60
61	62	63	64	65	66	67	68	69	70
71	72	73	74	75	76	77	78	79	80
81	82	83	84	85	86	87	88	89	90
91	92	93	94	95	96	97	98	99	100

Here are the numbers from one to one hundred in a number grid. This shows the one times table.

2 Times Table

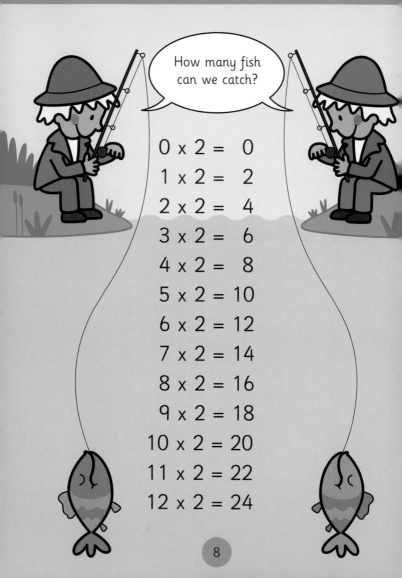

How many fish can we catch?

0 x 2 = 0
1 x 2 = 2
2 x 2 = 4
3 x 2 = 6
4 x 2 = 8
5 x 2 = 10
6 x 2 = 12
7 x 2 = 14
8 x 2 = 16
9 x 2 = 18
10 x 2 = 20
11 x 2 = 22
12 x 2 = 24

2 – two   2nd – second

Word	Meaning
double	two times as much
pair	two matching items
bicycle	two-wheeled cycle
twice	two times
twins	two children born at the same time

1	2	3	4	5	6	7	8	9	10
11	12	13	14	15	16	17	18	19	20
21	22	23	24	25	26	27	28	29	30
31	32	33	34	35	36	37	38	39	40
41	42	43	44	45	46	47	48	49	50
51	52	53	54	55	56	57	58	59	60
61	62	63	64	65	66	67	68	69	70
71	72	73	74	75	76	77	78	79	80
81	82	83	84	85	86	87	88	89	90
91	92	93	94	95	96	97	98	99	100

The numbers in blue show the pattern of the two times table. What do you notice about the numbers in the blue columns?

3 Times Table

0 x 3 =   0
1 x 3 =   3
2 x 3 =   6
3 x 3 =   9
4 x 3 = 12
5 x 3 = 15
6 x 3 = 18
7 x 3 = 21
8 x 3 = 24
9 x 3 = 27
10 x 3 = 30
11 x 3 = 33
12 x 3 = 36

How many mice are eating cheese?

3 – three   3rd – third

Word	Meaning
triple, treble	three times as much
tricycle	three-wheeled cycle
triangle	three-sided flat shape
trilogy	three part book, play or film
triplets	three children born at the same time

1	2	3	4	5	6	7	8	9	10
11	12	13	14	15	16	17	18	19	20
21	22	23	24	25	26	27	28	29	30
31	32	33	34	35	36	37	38	39	40
41	42	43	44	45	46	47	48	49	50
51	52	53	54	55	56	57	58	59	60
61	62	63	64	65	66	67	68	69	70
71	72	73	74	75	76	77	78	79	80
81	82	83	84	85	86	87	88	89	90
91	92	93	94	95	96	97	98	99	100

The numbers in red show the pattern of the three times table. What do you notice about the red numbers going downwards?

11

4 Times Table

$$0 \times 4 = 0$$
$$1 \times 4 = 4$$
$$2 \times 4 = 8$$
$$3 \times 4 = 12$$
$$4 \times 4 = 16$$
$$5 \times 4 = 20$$
$$6 \times 4 = 24$$
$$7 \times 4 = 28$$
$$8 \times 4 = 32$$
$$9 \times 4 = 36$$
$$10 \times 4 = 40$$
$$11 \times 4 = 44$$
$$12 \times 4 = 48$$

How many sides does my kite have?

4 – four   4th – fourth

Word	Meaning
quadruple	four times as much
quarter	one of four equal parts of a whole
square	a flat shape with four equal sides
quadruplets	four children born at the same time

1	2	3	4	5	6	7	8	9	10
11	12	13	14	15	16	17	18	19	20
21	22	23	24	25	26	27	28	29	30
31	32	33	34	35	36	37	38	39	40
41	42	43	44	45	46	47	48	49	50
51	52	53	54	55	56	57	58	59	60
61	62	63	64	65	66	67	68	69	70
71	72	73	74	75	76	77	78	79	80
81	82	83	84	85	86	87	88	89	90
91	92	93	94	95	96	97	98	99	100

The numbers in orange show the four times table. What do you notice about it?
Does it remind you of the two times table?

5 Times Table

0 x 5 = 0
1 x 5 = 5
2 x 5 = 10
3 x 5 = 15
4 x 5 = 20
5 x 5 = 25
6 x 5 = 30
7 x 5 = 35
8 x 5 = 40
9 x 5 = 45
10 x 5 = 50
11 x 5 = 55
12 x 5 = 60

How many stars are in the sky?

5 – five   5th – fifth

Word   **Meaning**

quintuple   five times as much

pentagon   a shape with five sides

quintet   five singers or musicians

pentathlon   an athletics contest with five events

1	2	3	4	5	6	7	8	9	10
11	12	13	14	15	16	17	18	19	20
21	22	23	24	25	26	27	28	29	30
31	32	33	34	35	36	37	38	39	40
41	42	43	44	45	46	47	48	49	50
51	52	53	54	55	56	57	58	59	60
61	62	63	64	65	66	67	68	69	70
71	72	73	74	75	76	77	78	79	80
81	82	83	84	85	86	87	88	89	90
91	92	93	94	95	96	97	98	99	100

The numbers in yellow show the five times table.
Look at the yellow columns. Do you notice
anything about the units?

6 Times Table

$0 \times 6 = 0$
$1 \times 6 = 6$
$2 \times 6 = 12$
$3 \times 6 = 18$
$4 \times 6 = 24$
$5 \times 6 = 30$
$6 \times 6 = 36$
$7 \times 6 = 42$
$8 \times 6 = 48$
$9 \times 6 = 54$
$10 \times 6 = 60$
$11 \times 6 = 66$
$12 \times 6 = 72$

How many spots does each butterfly have?

6 – six 6th – sixth

Word	Meaning
sextuple	six times as much
hexagon	a flat shape with six equal sides
sextuplets	six children born at the same time
sextet	six singers or musicians

1	2	3	4	5	6	7	8	9	10
11	12	13	14	15	16	17	18	19	20
21	22	23	24	25	26	27	28	29	30
31	32	33	34	35	36	37	38	39	40
41	42	43	44	45	46	47	48	49	50
51	52	53	54	55	56	57	58	59	60
61	62	63	64	65	66	67	68	69	70
71	72	73	74	75	76	77	78	79	80
81	82	83	84	85	86	87	88	89	90
91	92	93	94	95	96	97	98	99	100

The numbers in green show the six times table. What is the pattern of the numbers in the green squares?

7 Times Table

0 x 7 = 0
1 x 7 = 7
2 x 7 = 14
3 x 7 = 21
4 x 7 = 28
5 x 7 = 35
6 x 7 = 42
7 x 7 = 49
8 x 7 = 56
9 x 7 = 63
10 x 7 = 70
11 x 7 = 77
12 x 7 = 84

How many colours are in the rainbow?

7 – seven   7th – seventh

Word   **Meaning**

September   in Roman times, this was the
            seventh month of the year

septennial lasting for seven years

heptagon   a seven-sided flat shape

septet   seven singers or musicians

1	2	3	4	5	6	7	8	9	10
11	12	13	14	15	16	17	18	19	20
21	22	23	24	25	26	27	28	29	30
31	32	33	34	35	36	37	38	39	40
41	42	43	44	45	46	47	48	49	50
51	52	53	54	55	56	57	58	59	60
61	62	63	64	65	66	67	68	69	70
71	72	73	74	75	76	77	78	79	80
81	82	83	84	85	86	87	88	89	90
91	92	93	94	95	96	97	98	99	100

The numbers in yellow show the pattern of the
seven times table. What do you notice this time?

8 Times Table

$$0 \times 8 = 0$$
$$1 \times 8 = 8$$
$$2 \times 8 = 16$$
$$3 \times 8 = 24$$
$$4 \times 8 = 32$$
$$5 \times 8 = 40$$
$$6 \times 8 = 48$$
$$7 \times 8 = 56$$
$$8 \times 8 = 64$$
$$9 \times 8 = 72$$
$$10 \times 8 = 80$$
$$11 \times 8 = 88$$
$$12 \times 8 = 96$$

How many tentacles does an octopus have?

8 – eight 8th – eighth

Word   **Meaning**

October   in Roman times, this was the
             eighth month of the year

octagon   an eight-sided flat shape

octopus   a sea creature with eight tentacles

octet   eight singers or musicians

1	2	3	4	5	6	7	8	9	10
11	12	13	14	15	16	17	18	19	20
21	22	23	24	25	26	27	28	29	30
31	32	33	34	35	36	37	38	39	40
41	42	43	44	45	46	47	48	49	50
51	52	53	54	55	56	57	58	59	60
61	62	63	64	65	66	67	68	69	70
71	72	73	74	75	76	77	78	79	80
81	82	83	84	85	86	87	88	89	90
91	92	93	94	95	96	97	98	99	100

The numbers in blue show the pattern of the
eight times table. Can you see a pattern in the
numbers below the blue squares?

9 Times Table

0 x 9 =	0
1 x 9 =	9
2 x 9 =	18
3 x 9 =	27
4 x 9 =	36
5 x 9 =	45
6 x 9 =	54
7 x 9 =	63
8 x 9 =	72
9 x 9 =	81
10 x 9 =	90
11 x 9 =	99
12 x 9 =	108

How old am I today?

9 – nine   9th – ninth

Word

Meaning

November — in Roman times, this was the ninth month of the year

nonagon — nine-sided flat shape

nonet — nine singers or musicians

1	2	3	4	5	6	7	8	9	10
11	12	13	14	15	16	17	18	19	20
21	22	23	24	25	26	27	28	29	30
31	32	33	34	35	36	37	38	39	40
41	42	43	44	45	46	47	48	49	50
51	52	53	54	55	56	57	58	59	60
61	62	63	64	65	66	67	68	69	70
71	72	73	74	75	76	77	78	79	80
81	82	83	84	85	86	87	88	89	90
91	92	93	94	95	96	97	98	99	100

The numbers in pink show the pattern of the nine times table. What is the pattern of the tens? What is the pattern of the units?

10 Times Table

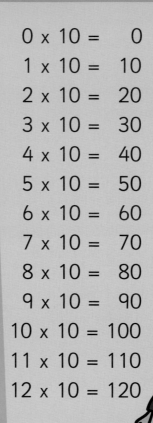

0 x 10 =   0
1 x 10 =   10
2 x 10 =   20
3 x 10 =   30
4 x 10 =   40
5 x 10 =   50
6 x 10 =   60
7 x 10 =   70
8 x 10 =   80
9 x 10 =   90
10 x 10 = 100
11 x 10 = 110
12 x 10 = 120

How many skittles are in the alley?

24

10 – ten   10th – tenth

Word	Meaning
December	in Roman times, this was the tenth month
decade	ten years
decagon	ten-sided shape
decathlon	an athletic contest with ten events

1	2	3	4	5	6	7	8	9	10
11	12	13	14	15	16	17	18	19	20
21	22	23	24	25	26	27	28	29	30
31	32	33	34	35	36	37	38	39	40
41	42	43	44	45	46	47	48	49	50
51	52	53	54	55	56	57	58	59	60
61	62	63	64	65	66	67	68	69	70
71	72	73	74	75	76	77	78	79	80
81	82	83	84	85	86	87	88	89	90
91	92	93	94	95	96	97	98	99	100

The numbers in blue show the ten times table.
What is the pattern of the tens?
What is the pattern of the units?

11 Times Table

0 x 11	=	0
1 x 11	=	11
2 x 11	=	22
3 x 11	=	33
4 x 11	=	44
5 x 11	=	55
6 x 11	=	66
7 x 11	=	77
8 x 11	=	88
9 x 11	=	99
10 x 11	=	110
11 x 11	=	121
12 x 11	=	132

11 – eleven 11th – eleventh

Word

hendecagon

Meaning

eleven-sided flat shape

1	2	3	4	5	6	7	8	9	10
11	12	13	14	15	16	17	18	19	20
21	22	23	24	25	26	27	28	29	30
31	32	33	34	35	36	37	38	39	40
41	42	43	44	45	46	47	48	49	50
51	52	53	54	55	56	57	58	59	60
61	62	63	64	65	66	67	68	69	70
71	72	73	74	75	76	77	78	79	80
81	82	83	84	85	86	87	88	89	90
91	92	93	94	95	96	97	98	99	100

The numbers in green show the eleven times table.
What do you notice about the tens and units?
Can you see a link with the one times table?

12 Times Table

$$0 \times 12 = 0$$
$$1 \times 12 = 12$$
$$2 \times 12 = 24$$
$$3 \times 12 = 36$$
$$4 \times 12 = 48$$
$$5 \times 12 = 60$$
$$6 \times 12 = 72$$
$$7 \times 12 = 84$$
$$8 \times 12 = 96$$
$$9 \times 12 = 108$$
$$10 \times 12 = 120$$
$$11 \times 12 = 132$$
$$12 \times 12 = 144$$

How many balls am I juggling?

12 – twelve 12th – twelfth

Word   **Meaning**

dodecagon   twelve-sided flat shape
dozen   twelve of something

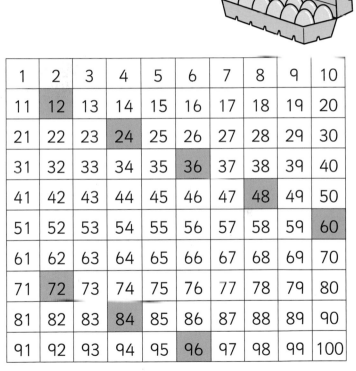

1	2	3	4	5	6	7	8	9	10
11	12	13	14	15	16	17	18	19	20
21	22	23	24	25	26	27	28	29	30
31	32	33	34	35	36	37	38	39	40
41	42	43	44	45	46	47	48	49	50
51	52	53	54	55	56	57	58	59	60
61	62	63	64	65	66	67	68	69	70
71	72	73	74	75	76	77	78	79	80
81	82	83	84	85	86	87	88	89	90
91	92	93	94	95	96	97	98	99	100

The numbers in purple show the twelve times
table. What is the pattern of the numbers
this time?

1 Times Table	2 Times Table	3 Times Table
0 x 1 = 0	0 x 2 = 0	0 x 3 = 0
1 x 1 = 1	1 x 2 = 2	1 x 3 = 3
2 x 1 = 2	2 x 2 = 4	2 x 3 = 6
3 x 1 = 3	3 x 2 = 6	3 x 3 = 9
4 x 1 = 4	4 x 2 = 8	4 x 3 = 12
5 x 1 = 5	5 x 2 = 10	5 x 3 = 15
6 x 1 = 6	6 x 2 = 12	6 x 3 = 18
7 x 1 = 7	7 x 2 = 14	7 x 3 = 21
8 x 1 = 8	8 x 2 = 16	8 x 3 = 24
9 x 1 = 9	9 x 2 = 18	9 x 3 = 27
10 x 1 = 10	10 x 2 = 20	10 x 3 = 30
11 x 1 = 11	11 x 2 = 22	11 x 3 = 33
12 x 1 = 12	12 x 2 = 24	12 x 3 = 36

7 Times Table	8 Times Table	9 Times Table
0 x 7 = 0	0 x 8 = 0	0 x 9 = 0
1 x 7 = 7	1 x 8 = 8	1 x 9 = 9
2 x 7 = 14	2 x 8 = 16	2 x 9 = 18
3 x 7 = 21	3 x 8 = 24	3 x 9 = 27
4 x 7 = 28	4 x 8 = 32	4 x 9 = 36
5 x 7 = 35	5 x 8 = 40	5 x 9 = 45
6 x 7 = 42	6 x 8 = 48	6 x 9 = 54
7 x 7 = 49	7 x 8 = 56	7 x 9 = 63
8 x 7 = 56	8 x 8 = 64	8 x 9 = 72
9 x 7 = 63	9 x 8 = 72	9 x 9 = 81
10 x 7 = 70	10 x 8 = 80	10 x 9 = 90
11 x 7 = 77	11 x 8 = 88	11 x 9 = 99
12 x 7 = 84	12 x 8 = 96	12 x 9 = 108